HOW TO SELF-PUBLISH ON AMAZON

The Essential Step-by-Step Guide to Publishing Success

C. GRAHAM CANN

Chas Cann Publishers

Dedicated to Greg and Ian

I am so proud to call you my sons

Contents

INTRODUCTION

I'm so pleased to welcome you to 'How to Self-Publish on Amazon: The Essential Step-By-Step Guide to Publishing Success'. In this book, we're going to be looking at all aspects of getting your book published on the Amazon platform, whether it's a Kindle e-book and/or a print version. We'll also touch on some of the ways that you can market your book not only on Amazon itself, but also via other platforms designed to increase sales.

To make certain that you have the greatest possible knowledge of self-publishing, we'll be:

- ensuring that your book cover is fit for purpose, which means maximising your sales

- looking at making an impact with the correct use of keywords and categories which are vital to attract potential readers to your book

- developing a book description that will leave your potential readers with no alternative but to click that BUY button

- easing the burden of formatting your book interior so you'll feel more confident that your readers will get what they're expecting

- looking at editing and proofreading to make your book the best it can be

Before you publish your book, these are the essential areas that need to be spot-on. You need to optimise these core areas of your book because, if you don't, any marketing you do will be totally ineffective - not only will you lose money with paid advertising, but also damage your confidence in the whole self-publishing process.

We'll also advise you on how much money you need to start this publishing project and what sort of earnings you can expect.

For those who'd like to take the entire plan to another level, we'll show where else you can publish your books and make effective strides globally in increasing your income, which needn't be determined by book sales alone. By becoming an author entrepreneur, a whole new vista is available to you with, for example, affiliate marketing, building and maintaining email lists and online course creation. We'll look at some of these potential income streams too. There's a whole new world of opportunity just waiting to be seized!

If this all seems too overwhelming, I want to reassure you I'm going to start at the beginning and guide you step-by-step in the publishing process, showing you what you need to do to make a success of your book. If you don't yet know what to write about, don't worry! I'll help you find profitable niches, which are subject areas that are selling well on Amazon. When you write your book, you want to know it's going to be on a topic that people are interested in and buying in numbers. The idea of writing a book, 'Underwater Macrame for Busy Mums' may excite **you**, but, spoiler alert, it won't make you much money. So, we'll establish a niche market that is selling well but, more importantly, one that you'll enjoy writing about because you need to be invested in your project emotionally and intellectually. It needs to interest you and be something you really want to write about.

We start the ball rolling with a chapter on how to set up and open your KDP account and then how to optimise your book, making it the best it can be, before uploading it on to Amazon. Yes, there will be aspects of self-publishing you'll need to master, but once you know how to do it, you can replicate it for every book. You can even teach others how to do it! Nobody wants to make a success of your book more than you. We'll work together to point you in the right direction, giving you sound and practical advice.

It doesn't matter if you haven't yet written a book or if you're a fairly established independent author but finding that your books just aren't selling too well. This book is about taking you from where you are right now, guiding you on how to get where you want to be, and showing you what's possible in the world of publishing and beyond.

For writers who just want to get a book published and are not concerned if it makes money or not, you'll also find a wealth of information in this book to get your manuscript uploaded on to the Amazon platform and finally be proud to see your name in print.

Last but not least, we have a section on setting your goals in the chapter 'Time Management'. These should inspire and motivate you. What do you want to achieve in the next ten years? How will you do it?

In addition, you'll notice as you read through the text that certain words or phrases have been underlined. If you need the web links to these, you can find them all via the 'Helpful Links' page at the back of this book.

I sincerely hope that this book will be a practical foundation for your entire writing career.

Here's to your success!

Note: There are affiliate links in this book to products I fully endorse and recommend – these are products that I have used, currently use or would use if there was a personal need. I earn a small commission *at no extra cost to you*, which helps my tea and coffee fund!

1

CREATING YOUR KDP ACCOUNT

The first thing we need to do is to create your account. Amazon won't activate your account immediately because it takes a while for the tax information to be verified, so we can do this before we tackle anything else.

If you already have an Amazon account, log in as usual.

If you don't have an Amazon account, go to KDP https://kdp.amazon.com/en_US/ and sign up, entering your name, address and a password. Agree to Amazon's Terms and Conditions.

You'll notice that a warning box will appear, stating your account information is incomplete. Click 'Update Now' and the three sections below will appear. Before you can publish any books on the Amazon platform, these need to be completed.

- **Author/Publisher Information.** This is straightforward.

- **Getting Paid.** There are three ways to get paid by Amazon: direct deposit, wire transfer or cheque. Except for direct deposits, there is a minimum threshold before Amazon will pay you. At the time of writing, you need to have royalties over $100 (£100) before Amazon will pay out.

- **Tax Information.** Amazon needs valid tax details from you wherever you live before you can progress further with your application. If you're a non-US self-publisher, the US Government may withhold 30% of your royalties. Depending on where you live or where your company is registered (not your nationality), there may be an arrangement in place. Fortunately, some countries like the UK, Canada and Germany have an agreement with the US administration, which means they are all exempt from any taxes. However, countries such as Australia (5%), Portugal (10%) and India (15%) are not.

To ensure that you are exempt, or at least pay less than the statutory 30%, you'll need to complete some forms. The American IRS (Internal Revenue Service) views all non-US authors as small businesses, so all you require is an EIN (Employer Identification Number) which you can apply for online or call the IRS direct. Once you have your number, update your KDP account. Now that you've completed this stage, depending on your circumstances, you will pay less tax to the US authorities or hopefully, no tax at all.

One other thing, you cannot have a separate account for your shopping needs and another for your Amazon business. Your Amazon account can only have one email address and phone number.

2

HOW MUCH INVESTMENT DO I NEED TO SUCCEED?

OK, so you've set up your Amazon account. Now, let's identify what sort of investment needs to be made. The good news is that you don't need large amounts of capital to succeed in self-publishing. The amount of financial investment varies with all types of small businesses.

Self-publishing a book on Amazon can literally cost you nothing at all except your time.

However tempting that looks, if you want to make sales and have a rewarding career with your writing, then an investment will be necessary. Again, it depends why you're doing what you're doing. You may write and publish a book because it's been your life's ambition to see your name in print. Maybe you're not at all concerned about making money from this venture and that's fine. You can put together a book for literally nothing and see it listed in the biggest bookshop in the world.

If your intention and desire is to build a long-term business, then costs will need to be incurred if you're going to compete seriously in the marketplace with large traditional publishing houses. Many of these costs will be down to individual choices. For example, do you want to format your book or do you find the whole thing way outside your comfort zone or expertise? You may want to hire someone to do it for you. If you're a graphic designer, for example, with years of experience of book cover design, I guess you'd be happy to create a book cover yourself.

I've listed here some costs involved for those committed to long-term writing careers. Please note that I deal with all the headings below in more detail later in this book.

Book Covers

When I first started producing books, I knew pretty much from the get-go that the covers needed to be produced professionally and that I'd need to pay for this. If you're going to make a career out of self-publishing, my advice is not to attempt a do-it-yourself cover unless you have experience of this. There's nothing more off-putting to a reader than seeing a sub-standard, amateur book cover design. Covers range from around $10 to $1500+.

ISBNs

Amazon will issue an ISBN for free with its print books. However, if you want your book to be distributed outside

Amazon, I would strongly suggest buying your own ISBNs at the outset. You can start with a free ISBN from Amazon and change to the paid option further down the road if you wish. You can see the costs of ISBNs in the chapter 'Metadata and Why It's So Important'.

Formatting

I was in the process of building a publishing business and so it made sense to get to grips with formatting a book and not farming it out for others to do. This way I'd understand the whole thing from start to finish, but I have to say that it was, at best, frustrating and, at worst, extremely demanding and stressful. On saying that, I'm glad I stuck with it and, despite a huge learning curve, I still continue to do this job with every book. $30 - $300+ for a basic book with no images.

Sales Descriptions

There is an art to these and you can pay from $50 to $300+. You're paying for someone to formulate ad copy, which, if done correctly, will sell a lot more books.

Editing

If you require the services of an editor, you're looking somewhere between $300 and $2000.

Remember, this is an investment where you will expect a return on that outlay through sales of your books.

Each book is an asset that will pay you for the rest of your days and between 50 and 70 years after you die.

3

HOW MUCH CAN I EXPECT TO EARN?

When we talk about earnings, we're concentrating on your royalties from the Amazon KDP platform. There are a myriad of ways to earn money from book publishing. By going wide (or choosing to distribute your books beyond Amazon) can open up a whole new world of opportunity. Building email lists, selling e-books from your website, affiliate links, podcasts, YouTube videos, online courses, to name a few, can all enhance your earning abilities. For now, let's keep to Amazon and look at their commission payments.

Amazon pays you approximately 60 days after the end of the month in which the sales were reported. So, for example, Amazon will pay royalties received in January at the end of March.

KDP E-Book Royalties

E-books are arguably the most lucrative of all the formats. Amazon digitally produces these to be read on e-book readers such as Kindle and Nobo (Barnes and Noble). One e-book reader can hold hundreds of books, which make it compact and easy to use. Amazon has a royalty sweet-spot between $2.99 and $9.99, within which the royalty rate is 70% in most English-speaking countries. Outside this range, the lower rate of 35% is applied, in other words all books that retail below $2.99 and above $9.99.

If you opt for the 70% royalty rate, then Amazon charges $0.15 per megabyte (MB) on your file size after it's converted, which tends to be lower than the book's actual file size. There is no charge if you choose the 35% rate. This delivery fee will vary from country to country and you can see these rates on your KDP pricing page, which is the last page when you upload your book.

You'll notice from your pricing page that some countries charge VAT for books and this has to be considered when you calculate your commission. Fortunately, the US, UK and Canada have no such taxation, but if you have a presence in Europe (except Ireland), for example, then VAT is added to the cost of books in that region. Therefore, to work out your royalty, use this calculation:

70% commission x list price - VAT - delivery fee = royalty

35% commission x list price - VAT = royalty

KDP Print Royalties (Paperback and Hardback)

There are three things to consider when publishing a print version of your book, as they all affect the price.

1. The total number of pages

2. The type of paper you're using (i.e. standard colour, premium colour or black and white)

3. Where you wish to publish your book

The royalty for a print version of your book is 60% and the way to calculate your book's royalty is:

List Price x 60% - printing costs = royalty.

So, if your book retails at $6.99, the cost of printing your book is $1.93, you'll earn $2.26 (0.60 x 6.99 − 1.93 = 2.26). These figures are all worked out for you on each individual book on your KDP pricing page. Trim size, bleed settings and cover finish do not affect the printing costs.

Occasionally, Amazon will reduce the price of your book out of the blue. One reason may be to beat the price of one of their competitors. Even if they reduce the retail price of your book, you will still receive the same royalty.

Aim to make at least $2 profit on each book and you can see that selling just 10 books a day from e-book and paperback sales can realise around $600 per month which doesn't even include earnings from Kindle Unlimited, other formats like hard covers, large print and audiobooks. For many people, earning $600 per month, part-time, is not a trivial amount.

4
TIME MANAGEMENT

If we were all blessed with 48 hours in a day, wouldn't that make life easier? Probably not! Because we'd aim to fill all those extra hours with even more stuff and experience massive burn-out! The fact is, every man and woman on this planet has the same amount of time. The key to being productive and successful is how we use that time.

Finding More Time to Write

We can be very good at telling others and ourselves that we haven't got the hours in the day to write and yet find two or three hours a night watching Netflix and catching up with friends on Facebook. Many people in today's hectic world try to keep those plates spinning - juggling work, friends and family, domestic chores, hobbies and many other obligations.

However, you can always find time if you're passionate and committed. Joanna Penn, author and influencer, said: 'Back when I had a day job, I would write between 5am and 6am, then go to work, and in the evenings, I'd spend an hour or so after dinner podcasting, connecting with authors, dealing with email and social media, reading books and taking courses to learn new skills.'

It's all about setting your priorities. The number one priority is to find the time to write. Most authors do not write full time, so it has to be fitted in around their current responsibilities. Many find that writing in the morning is when they are the most alert and energised. Try waking up an hour or two earlier, before the rest of your household, so you can find some uninterrupted time. If you're more of a night owl, start when everyone else has gone to bed. That way, you can devote an hour or two of time solely to writing.

Ask yourself: 'Could I spend less time on social media, gaming and watching streaming services such as Netflix?' By saving just a couple of hours a week and devote that time to writing, you could achieve 1000 words. Do this for a full year and you have 52,000 words in your manuscript, enough for a novel.

Whatever block of time you can devote to writing, ensure that you commit to it intentionally. Nothing will get in the way of this time of day that you have agreed with yourself. It's not about waiting until you feel like writing. It's about starting at your given time of day and writing, whether or not you're feeling in the mood for it. Some days may be more productive than others. That's fine because, at the very least, you will have created something in your allotted time.

I know authors who write when they're waiting for a train to arrive or in a doctor's waiting room. They'll jot down their thoughts on their mobile device or in a notebook.

Essentially, we are all different and what works for one writer may not work for another. You will find the best way of working that suits you best.

Tracking Your Time

On the one hand, this can be a real pain to do, but on the other, it can reveal to you precisely where the hours go in a day. Often, we think we're being productive until we get the stark facts from such an exercise as this. Be honest with yourself and note down every activity in, say, a fifteen-minute period from the time you wake up to the time you go to bed. Track your activity for a week. This can be a great help in assessing how long you spend in every area of activity in your life and, ultimately, where you can fine-tune this process to be more productive.

Is there anything you could do more of? Conversely, is there anything you could do less of?

Distractions

These can cost you a lot of time. It can take 10 - 20 minutes to get back into the flow again after being side-tracked by something like answering the phone. I turn off my mobile during the times I've set aside for writing and I let landline calls go to voicemail. If you need to, wear headphones in order to shut out any noise that's going to distract you.

Time is valuable, especially if you're working full-time besides writing, so be protective of it. Ensure you maintain a level of focus on your work for the entire block of time that you've devoted to writing. Distractions aren't the sole domain of the external world. Many come from your internal realm. For example, while you're writing, you suddenly remember that you haven't bought a present for your grandson's birthday. Keep a notepad near your writing area so you can jot it down quickly and resume your writing straight away without succumbing to going online to buy the gift!

Batching

This is a useful time management tool where you're doing the same type of activity for large amounts of time which, for many authors, ranges from two hours to half a day. Batching means spending that time on **one task,** like concentrating on the first draft of your book. It doesn't mean writing ad copy, checking emails or researching marketing techniques! It's been proven that 'context-switching' - switching quickly between different tasks - can waste 40% of your productive time! Pick a length of time that suits you and use this to focus 100% on that one task.

Refresh

We are not machines. Some authors choose to write for longer periods of time during the day over a period of, say, 2-3 weeks in order to complete an entire book, but writing for hours and hours without a break can be counter-productive. Many use the Pomodoro Technique. You write for 25 minutes and then take a break for 5 minutes to do something totally unrelated, like exercising, meditation or doing a household chore. After four breaks (i.e. after 2 hours) take a 15 to 30-minute break. Keep lunch breaks to under an hour as you can lose the essential writing flow if it's any longer.

Don't forget to drink adequate amounts of water (men - 3 litres, women - 2.2 litres) which helps with your cognitive abilities.

Some writers take a week off between projects to recharge their batteries and prepare for the next book.

Motivate Yourself With Goal Setting

Setting goals can be a terrific motivator and keep you on track. Whereas at work you're acting under your boss's instructions, as a writer you have to be proactive and setting goals helps you with direction and stops you from becoming a rudderless ship. For example, your target is writing four hours a week every week with a view to achieving 500 words an hour – that's 2000 words a week or 26,000 words in 3 months. Using the acronym SMART is a handy reminder of what the key aspects of goal setting are:

SPECIFIC – They need to be precise and not wishy-washy. 'I'm going to write a book this year' is too vague. But 'I'm going to complete my first draft by 30th June and publish by 31st October' is more defined.

MEASURABLE – Saying that you want to improve your marketing means that it's difficult to quantify, but stating that you'll take a course on Amazon Ads means you can measure your marketing against having taken this course.

ATTAINABLE – You have to be realistic, but at the same time, the goal must stretch you to go beyond what you thought was possible. To write a full-length novel in a week, working on it in your spare time, is asking a lot, but to write a full-length novel in 6 months is achievable.

RELEVANT – Any sub-goal should serve the major goal. For instance, if your ten-year goal is to write twenty books, then your yearly goals need to reflect that. You'll hit your major goals only if you break these down to yearly, monthly, and daily targets.

TIME BOUND – There needs to be a deadline for your goals. I will read this book on how to write non-fiction by 30th April. Otherwise, other things get in the way or you forget and nothing is accomplished.

5

FINDING YOUR TARGET AUDIENCE

One of the first pre-requisites of publishing a book is to know your audience. An easy trap to fall into is to believe that your book, whether fiction or non-fiction, will appeal to everybody. It won't. Don't be ensnared by this point of view. There will be a specific audience for your book and these are the readers that need to be kept in your sights.

These are the people most likely to be interested in your book. When your audience sense that you're speaking directly to them, the more likely you are to convert them into customers. Everything about your book, including your cover, writing style and other metadata (see Chapter 7), should speak to your audience.

First, check out other books that are in the same genre as yours. By making a list of the top five best-selling authors and titles, checking out their covers and 'Look Insides', you'll get an idea who your potential readers will be. Do these authors have websites? If so, look for their blogs to discover what they're writing about, who's connecting with them and what they're saying.

Social media is a great resource by joining groups and online communities that have the same interests. This is where your audience will congregate. What are they posting about? These posts will give you clues about your potential readers. Search Facebook for groups interested in books like yours. Look for followers of your book's genre on Twitter and search for tweets that contain related hashtags.

Don't forget to look at any secondary audience. A book on Mindfulness may attract people who are experiencing anxiety and lacking inner peace, but it may also attract mindfulness teachers and educators.

Google searches will unearth where your target audience is already connecting and taking part in communities, blogs and networks.

Later on, we'll be looking at building your email list and as this list grows, you'll be able to survey your followers to discover more about them, such as their gender, where they live, what their interests and hobbies are and suchlike. By doing this, you'll build up a detailed analysis of your audience.

6
FINDING PROFITABLE NICHES

You may be thinking right now that you're uncertain what to write about or that you may have the seed of an idea but are not entirely sure if it would sell well. Either way, don't worry. That's what this chapter is all about - helping you to find a topic or niche that you would enjoy writing about and, one that will sell well and earn you good royalties.

We'll be highlighting niches in the market where large numbers of readers are showing an interest and are, therefore, prepared to buy. If huge numbers of people are buying these particular books, then surely, if you're looking to profit from your writing, these will be the topics you would favour. However, choosing a niche that doesn't get your creative juices flowing is counter-productive. You may find a topic that's selling terrifically well but doesn't interest you one little bit, so where's the pleasure in that? In this chapter, we'll find niches that are selling well **and** that resonate with you.

NON-FICTION

Make a List of Ten Hot Topics

In order to seek out those niches, head for www.amazon.com. Below the Amazon logo on the left, click 'All', opt for 'Kindle E-readers and Books' and under 'Kindle Store' click on 'Kindle Books'. Click on 'Best Sellers and More' and then 'Kindle Best Sellers'. Choose the category 'Top 100 Paid'. You now have in front of you the 100 best-selling Kindle titles in America. These are, at this moment in time, the most popular books on Amazon's largest marketplace.

Next, click 'Kindle eBooks' on the left-hand side and this opens up a list of categories from 'Art and Photography' to 'Travel'. When you click on, say, 'Health, Fitness and Dieting', this will reveal the Top 100 books on this subject. You can drill down further by clicking on the sub-categories like 'Nutrition' to discover the Top 100 best-selling titles in these as well. You can also use these categories and sub-categories to find ones that resonate with you - ones that you'll enjoy writing about. For example, as you click through all these hundreds of categories, you may like the category 'Self Help', so you click on it and discover 'Stress Management'. This appeals to you because of an episode in your life where you could identify how stress made you feel, the low points, how you were physically affected and the way you overcame it.

Now, check out the Top 100 books in this 'Stress Management' category, making a list of topics or keywords that crop up most as you browse through the titles. For instance, 'decluttering the mind', 'procrastination', 'happiness' may all feature several times as you go through each title in the Top 50. Bear in mind that you may find some books are more generalised and a specific topic is hard to find. Write down those topics that you've found several times in the titles. Try a different category and go through the same routine. You need to come up with 10 different ideas or topics on which to base your next book.

Now that you have these, take each one and ask yourself, 'What is the primary keyword that potential readers would insert in the Amazon search bar?' When you've found it, head over to www.amazon.com and type in that word. As you do so, Amazon will come up with other suggestions that people have actually typed into the search bar. The keyword you chose most likely comprised one word (or a short-tailed keyword) like 'happiness' but you can see that the suggestions that have been auto-generated have more than one word and are called long-tailed keywords like 'happiness at work' and 'happiness diet'. These may give you ideas and a different perspective on planning the title, sub-title, and the content of your book.

Is This Niche Profitable?

First, go into Incognito Mode which, if you're using Google Chrome, you need to click on the ellipsis in the top right-hand corner and click 'New Incognito Window'. This will ensure Chrome doesn't skew the results by previous searches you may have made on your Amazon account. Type 'happiness' into Amazon's search bar and start looking at books on the first three pages. Scroll down to the 'Product details'. Here you'll discover Amazon's Best Sellers Rank (ASBR), which you can see in the diagram below.

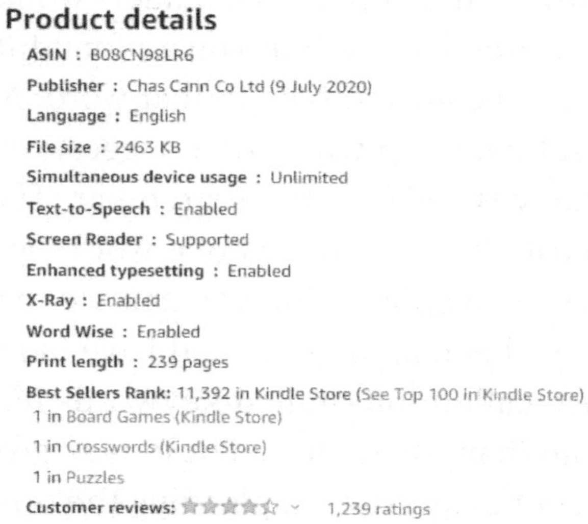

Product details

ASIN : B08CN98LR6

Publisher : Chas Cann Co Ltd (9 July 2020)

Language : English

File size : 2463 KB

Simultaneous device usage : Unlimited

Text-to-Speech : Enabled

Screen Reader : Supported

Enhanced typesetting : Enabled

X-Ray : Enabled

Word Wise : Enabled

Print length : 239 pages

Best Sellers Rank: 11,392 in Kindle Store (See Top 100 in Kindle Store)
   1 in Board Games (Kindle Store)
   1 in Crosswords (Kindle Store)
   1 in Puzzles

Customer reviews: ★★★★☆ ˅   1,239 ratings

This figure determines how well the book is selling. You're looking for a figure of 50,000 or less, which is a good indication that the book is selling well - the lower the figure, the better it's selling.

This will show you how well your keyword is doing in the e-book section of Amazon. Do the same exercise in the 'Books' (print version) section. Some books that don't sell very well on Kindle, do much better in paperback, so it's worth taking the time to see if there's a marked difference in favour of the print version. If so, you know your book will do better as a paperback than it will as an e-book.

Narrow down your original list of 10 niches to just one in terms of which ones are making the most money and, crucially, which ones you have the most passion about.

FICTION

Find Your Favoured Niche

Fiction is a very large and profitable sector for authors with a huge amount of sub-genres. For example, 'Science Fiction and Fantasy' has over forty sub-genres ranging from 'alien invasion' to 'superhero'.

The first thing to tackle, like non-fiction, is to ask: 'Which sub-genre am I more interested in?' I suggest making a list of each one that you favour. Second, your next list is your knowledge base in relation to these genres. Write about what you know. An example of your knowledge base could be that you've read a sub-genre extensively, which means you'll be aware of readers' expectations. You may also have worked at a place that would add value to your story line. By expanding your knowledge base, you'll have far more input into the novel and reduce some research time.

Are Books in Your Genre Making Money?

Once you have aligned your preferential sub-genre to your knowledge base, let's find out whether your selected sector has the potential to make you money. Following the same strategy as we did in Non-Fiction, go to Incognito Mode and then type the sub-genre (e.g. 'Cyberpunk Science Fiction') into the Kindle e-book search bar. Check out the first three pages of books, looking at the Amazon Best-Seller Rank for each of the books. Are they selling well in your sub-genre or not? This will give you a clue about how each book is faring in the marketplace and if you can make money.

Once you've completed this task, do the same again in 'Books'.

Saving Time and Effort

It's always good to do this manually at least once to get a feel of the whole method, but there is a way to do this niche research in a matter of minutes. Publisher Rocket will save you many hours that you can better devote to your writing. It comes with a very reasonable price tag and will pay for itself in terms of saved time.

Add the word 'happiness', for instance, to Rocket's search bar in 'Competition Analyzer' and you can decide whether you search for Kindle or Books in the US, UK or Germany. Hit 'Go Get Em Rocket!' and you will see on your screen all the books on 'happiness'. Rocket will show you how old the book is, its ASBR ranking, estimated monthly sales and more. At a glance, you can see whether or not a niche is profitable.

	Title	Type	Author	Age	ABSR	# Of Pages	KWT	Price	DY Sales	MO Sales	
	The Happiness Advantage How a Positive Brain Fuels Success in Work and Life	eBook See the Categories	Shawn Achor	4279	30788	258	Yes	$13.99	$137	$3.154	Check it out
	The Art of Happiness, 10th Anniversary Edition A Handbook for Living	eBook See the Categories	Dalai Lama	4627	49534	364	Yes	$14.99	$77	$1,764	Check it out
	Happiness Essential Mindfulness Practices	eBook See the Categories	Thich Nhat Hanh	6161	244581	178	Yes	$12.99	$0	$169	Check it out
	The Happiness Trap How to Stop Struggling and Start Living	eBook See the Categories	Russ Harris	5112	29586	258	Yes	$13.99	$141	$3,251	Check it out

7

METADATA AND WHY IT'S SO IMPORTANT

You may have heard the word 'metadata' being bandied about in the publishing world. This is simply any data that describes your book. It connects your content to your prospective readers. So, what would that be? It's any information that leads prospects to your book. It's quite wide-ranging and includes your book title and subtitle, cover, book description, keywords, categories, ISBN and pricing. These are critically important because if they're done correctly, your book sales will grow exponentially.

Book Cover

The phrase 'never judge a book by its cover' is **not** one that's used in book publishing circles because readers **always** judge a book by its cover. It's one of your core selling points and to scrimp and save by designing your own can be a recipe for disaster. Why? Readers are not stupid. They're tuned in to certain genre covers. If your cover does not come up to their expectations, they will pass it by. This is especially true of fiction. 'But', I hear you say 'I've spent hours working on my cover and I really like it'. The hard truth is that it doesn't matter whether **you** like it. It's ultimately down to whether your readers like it – they're the ones about to buy your book, not **you**! Sorry to be harsh, but it has to be genre specific and aimed at your target audience.

To be honest, readers can usually tell a DIY cover from a mile away and they equate home-made covers with poorly written and below par books. They simply won't give them a second look. Yes, it will cost you money for a professional cover. At the top of the tree are professional designers who, if you choose one wisely, will know what works in your genre. They have years of experience knowing what works and what doesn't. They know about light, balance, shadow, typography, perspective and blending. An excellent resource is the <u>Alliance of Independent Authors (ALLi)</u> which has listings of specially selected professional book cover designers.

You can spend hundreds of dollars on top-notch professionals, but if your budget doesn't stretch to that, there are resources like <u>Upwork</u> or <u>Fiverr</u> who will do an excellent job for you, depending on who you choose. I've worked with a lady on Fiverr for years. She is a 'Top Rated Seller' with over 1000 five-star ratings to her name and she has produced some fine covers. But she doesn't create them from scratch. I check out some best-selling books in my genre and supply two covers from books that are selling well and then choose up to three photos from a photo website that are then incorporated into the cover. The good news is that you can change aspects of the cover (revisions) until you get it just how you want it. One cover my designer created is now a #1 best-seller, so don't listen to anyone who berates designers in this 'cheaper' end of the market. See my blog on how to find impressive book cover designers on Fiverr. If you want a cover created from scratch, that will be at the higher end of the spectrum.

Book Description

The book description is the blurb you find on your sales page on Amazon near the book cover photo. It's what you include on your Details Page when you upload your book. This is an important section and is not something that should be disregarded or completed as an afterthought. Your cover has attracted your potential readers, and the purpose of the description is to give them a reason to buy your book. The book description is not a summary of your book. It is more of a sales pitch. Readers have to be persuaded that your book and no-one else's is the one that they're going to purchase. OK, so how do you do this?

Non-Fiction

Here's an example from 'The New Puppy Handbook: Your Easy Step-by-Step Guide to Choosing, Training and Caring for Your Puppy':

When you have made the decision to introduce a puppy into your home, you may be naturally apprehensive, particularly if you are becoming a pet parent for the first time.

Are you sure you know the best place to obtain your puppy?
Do you know for certain what supplies and equipment you are going to need?
How are you going to housebreak and train your puppy?

In this **detailed manual**, *'The New Puppy Handbook'*, Christian de Silva shares a **comprehensive knowledge of puppy management.**

This long-awaited **step-by-step guide to choosing, training and caring for your puppy** will be all that you need. By following and putting into practice what you read in this book, **you will be preparing your new arrival for a long and happy life and, in addition, you will become more confident day by day.**

In *'The New Puppy Handbook'* you will discover:
- **How to choose your puppy and the potential pitfalls** avoiding costly mistakes
- **Preparing your home and garden for your new arrival will give you peace of mind**
- **Shopping for supplies and equipment knowing that you have everything you need from day one**
- **Training your new puppy correctly will lead to a happy, well-adjusted adult canine**
- **Caring and looking after your puppy every day creating an unbreakable bond**

To raise a healthy and well-behaved puppy, just scroll up the page and click the BUY NOW button

With non-fiction (and fiction), it's all about hooking the reader with your first words. Don't give your browsing reader the opportunity to click elsewhere. The Amazon sales page reveals only the first few lines of your description initially, so it has to be good to be noticed straight away. The reader has to click on 'See More' to read the rest. In the first line, the reader is hooked because what new puppy owner will not be apprehensive? It then presents questions that potential new puppy owners may be anxious about. Find out their pain points. What are the key problems your book will solve? By listing them, usually as three questions, you're communicating to your reader that you understand their predicament and empathise with them.

Say something about the credentials of the author and then explain how your book will solve the problems they currently have. In non-fiction, we achieve this by using around five bullet points. The first part of the bullet point is giving facts about what the book will do for the reader. A benefit follows the fact - 'What's it going to do for me?'

For example:

'Preparing your home and garden for your new arrival' is FACT. '...giving you peace of mind' is a BENEFIT. Follow the facts with a benefit so readers can clearly see how they'll feel as a result of preparing their home and garden.

People tend to scan descriptions so, highlighting the odd relevant phrase in bold type will enhance the major points that you want the potential reader to engage with.

End with a Call to Action (CTA). This is an action that you want the reader to take!

Fiction

It's the same with fiction. You're not writing a synopsis of the book but explaining to the reader the journey they're going to make. The first point of focus is hooking the reader with something that piques their interest. This is the most important sentence in the whole description. Many authors put the first line in bold and also the last line or Call to Action, but rarely do you use bold in a fiction description.

Next, establish the time, settings and genre style. Then bring in the protagonist who is likeable, who the reader relates to and why they need to follow this character.

The next paragraph is for raising the stakes – the power struggle that is going to ensue between the antagonist and the hero.

The following paragraph has got to leave the reader wanting more.

The concluding paragraph includes a Call to Action (CTA).

Keywords

Amazon is the third largest search engine in the world. Every day, readers are searching for books like yours. Relevant keywords will help those readers find your book. But how do you find the right keywords?

On the 'Details Page' on KDP, you'll find spaces for seven keywords. Your title and subtitle should be full of keywords. Any keywords in your title and subtitle don't need to be repeated here, which leaves you free to find some fresh, exciting words that best describe your book.

One way to do this is to go into 'Incognito Mode' on your PC or tablet. To do this on Chrome, click on the ellipsis in the top right-hand corner and open 'New Incognito Window'. By doing this, your search won't be influenced by anything you've been browsing for or by cookies and site data. Type the word, say, 'meditation' into the search bar and see what auto-populates underneath. When I tried it on www.ama zon.com under 'Books', this came up:

meditations **marcus aurelius**

meditation

meditations **the annotated edition**

meditation **books**

meditation **journal**

meditation **diary**

meditation **planner**

meditation **and yoga fundamentals**

meditation**s gregory hays**

meditation **for busy people**

These are actual searches that readers have typed into the search bar. What you're looking for are relevant keywords that apply to your book. For example, 'meditation for busy people' could well describe your book. Next, type in 'meditation a' in the search bar and see what comes up. Is there anything here that looks like a good fit? Now do another search by typing in 'meditation b' and so on till you reach the end of the alphabet. What have you discovered? A bunch of words that you can use as your keywords.

You now have a list of relevant keywords that people type into the search bar of the Amazon website. What the data doesn't tell you is how popular they are. Some of these keywords may get a huge amount of searches but no-one buys from them so we need to look at keywords that are actually making sales.

Find the top three books that line up with one keyword on your list. Pick one book and check out its 'Best-Seller Rank' (BSR). To find the BSR, scroll down from the book cover on the Amazon sales page until you reach 'Product Details'.

This will show if the keyword or phrase for that book is actually selling. If the BSR is 50,000, you know the book is selling reasonably well. Go below this figure and the income from sales will increase. So, we're looking for a BSR of 50,000 and under. Repeat for the other two books in the top three and then continue the process for all your keywords.

So, using this strategy, you can now see clearly which keywords shoppers are using and which ones sell. The last part of the puzzle is to assess how competitive those keywords are. How do we do this? It involves some detective work.

Statistically, if your book shows up at number one in the rankings for that keyword, you are far more likely to get the sale. As you head down the rankings, your chances decrease, so what we have to do is achieve a high ranking. In order to do this, check out books in the top ten rankings for your keyword/phrase:

- Book Covers – covers are key to getting book sales, but is your competitor's cover below average but still attracting sales? That's good for you if your cover is far better

- Titles and Sub-titles – is the keyword in the title or sub-title of your competitor's book?

- Reviews – what review rating do they have and how

many reviews? Are they recent reviews? Low and poor reviews will be a sign that your book can do better

- Age – is it an old book and still selling in large quantities? This will be difficult to compete with

- Book Descriptions – is yours going to seal the deal more than your competitors?

We now know if your chosen keywords are 1) popular, 2) selling well and 3) competitive. By the time you've completed the keyword search, you'll have seven top keywords at your fingertips.

Phew! Yes, doing this manually takes time, but it remains a viable option if you're just starting out. As I've already mentioned, Publisher Rocket saves an enormous amount of time, which is a resource that we can ill afford to waste. Publisher Rocket does much more than just deliver keyword data. It also has tabs where you can check out your competitors, search categories and look up Amazon Ad keywords.

There are seven keyword spaces to fill when you upload a book to Amazon. They can range from one up to 50 characters, which include spaces. There's no need to repeat any of the keywords that you've already used in the book title and sub-title because Amazon's algorithm uses those anyway.

One proven formula that Dave Chesson of Kindlepreneur tested successfully in these seven keyword boxes is this: in four of the seven boxes, add a strong, relevant keyword (or keyword phrases) in each. For the other three boxes, use all 50 characters (or near enough) with various keywords and phrases not already used. Amazon will use any combination of these words to tie in with a keyword phrase a shopper has entered.

Categories

Categories are the sections of the Amazon store where customers can discover your book. Think of them as the different areas of a physical bookstore (crime, history, science fiction and so on). Choosing the right book categories can have an enormous impact on whether or not your book becomes a #1 Amazon Best-Seller.

Amazon changed the rules on categories in May 2023. In the past you could choose two BISAC categories of which there were around 4,800 in total and then you could increase that figure to ten categories. All you had to do was to contact KDP asking them to add more for you from Amazon's list of categories, which amounted to more than 11,000.

Now, when you set up your book details on KDP prior to publishing, they invite you to choose just three Amazon categories with no option to add more. On the 'Details

Page' on KDP, you'll see the place where you need to add your categories.

It's always a good policy to check out your competitors on any number of issues and not least what categories their books fall under. So, how do you find out all the categories that your competitors' books are linked to? There are 2 ways to do this:

- Publisher Rocket. This software will show you in seconds the book categories of any Amazon book, which means you now know what categories your competitors have opted for. Not only that, but it shows you how many sales a day you'll need to make to become a #1 best-seller in any category. The image below shows what happens when you click 'Unleash the Categories' in the 'Competition Analyzer'. This is where you can find every category your competitors' books are listed under. One of the new features of Publisher Rocket includes a list of keywords relevant to each category. In this example, you can see just some of the categories listed when I typed 'habits' into the search bar.

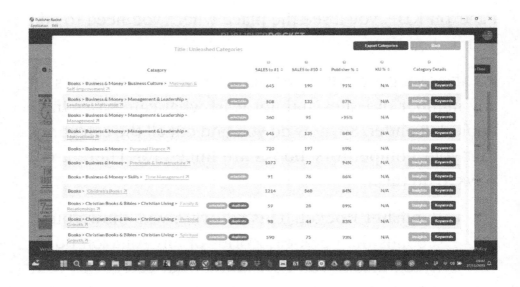

- The second way to check your competitors' book categories is <u>Bklnk</u>, a free resource where, at the time of writing, you can check categories in the US, UK, Germany and Canada. Enter the book's ASIN or ISBN-10 (the ten-figure ISBN) in the space provided, select the country of the Amazon store and click 'GO FIND!' and you'll see them displayed. You can insert your own book's details to check your own book categories.

Check each string or sequence of categories and sub-categories in the Kindle **and** print versions because they will be different. Don't forget to do this exercise for each country too. A string or sequence will look something like this:

Kindle Store>Kindle eBooks>Self-Help>Eating Disorders & Body Image.

ISBNs

What is an ISBN?

It's an acronym for International Standard Book Number and every single print version will have one. You can find it embedded in the barcode on the back cover and usually on the copyright page. It allows bookshops, online retailers, distributors, wholesalers and libraries to classify books, analyse sales data and facilitate stock control.

Do I Actually Need an ISBN For My Books?

It depends. If your plans are to publish solely on one platform, such as Amazon, then you can use their free ISBNs for print versions and ASINs (Amazon Standard Identification Number) for e-books.

However, if you're planning to go wide (publish your books on a range of different platforms like Apple, Kobo and Ingram Spark), my advice would be to buy your own ISBNs for e-books **and** print at the outset if you're able to.

If you choose to use your own ISBNs, then you'll need to purchase them. Canadian citizens are in the fortunate position of being able to acquire them for free. ISBNs are country specific so if you live in the UK, you'd buy yours from

Nielsen's (https://www.nielsenisbnstore.com/). Authors in the US would purchase theirs from Bowker's (https://www.bowker.com/). Check out this website for ISBN agencies in all other countries – https://www.isbn-international.org/content/national-isbn-agencies.

Remember, you'll need a different ISBN for paperbacks, hardbacks, large print versions, e-books (preferably) and audiobooks. Buying individual ISBNs works out very expensive. If you plan on writing many books, then decide on what quantity you require and can afford. The more you buy, the cheaper they become.

At the time of writing, these are the quantities and prices for Bowker and Nielsen:

BOWKER (USA):

1 – $125

10 – $295

100 – $575

NIELSEN (UK):

1 – £91

10 – £174

100 – £379

Once you've bought ISBNs, they will not expire.

Be wary of purchasing ISBNs from third parties. The imprint (or ISBN ownership) remains forever with the purchaser of the ISBN. They will be recognised as the publisher, **not you**, which can cause problems.

8
FORMATTING

What is formatting? In order for the interior of your book to have a recognised structure and to meet your readers' expectations, it needs to be formatted correctly. Readers can view the interior of your book via 'Look Inside' and can assess what the book looks like. Sub-standard formatting puts off many readers, not to mention poor grammar and punctuation mistakes.

When I first started on my self-publishing journey, this was the most challenging area for me, but like anything in life, if you're prepared to persevere, it becomes a lot easier. Let's be honest, formatting is an essential part of getting your book published. Readers know instinctively what a well-formatted book looks like and not only that, but you're often going head-to-head with large traditional publishing houses who have been doing this successfully for years.

I realised quickly that I had two choices. Either I placed the manuscript with someone who would do the job for me or I learnt how to do it myself. For me, I was determined to learn how to do this. One reason was that I wanted to keep my costs down, particularly in the early days. Another reason for doing it myself was that if I needed to make any corrections like adding new books to the back matter, I didn't want to pay for this service every time. Finally, I knew that by understanding the process fully, I could pass this knowledge on to others in the future.

How do you want to proceed?

Here are some suggestions for getting the job done:

MICROSOFT WORD: You can format in MS Word for e-books and print versions but this software can be a bit of a headache unless you know what you're doing. After much trial and error and seeing red on many occasions, I have learnt most of its eccentricities and we are now friends!

USING KDP TEMPLATES: Pre-loaded Word templates allow you to create your paperback/hardback with most of the work done for you. You can copy and paste chapters from your Word/Google document direct into a template. You can download blank templates or templates with sample content at https://kdp.amazon.com/en_US/help/topic/ G201834230 which acts as a useful guide.

KINDLE CREATE: With e-books, you can use Kindle Create, which is a free formatting tool from Amazon. I wasn't overly impressed, to be fair. I find it very basic and lacking in choice, but for a very rudimentary e-book, this would be a good option. https://kdp.amazon.com/en_US/help/topic /G202187830

REEDSY: The Reedsy Book Editor is a free formatting tool which comes from a well-established and respected company in the industry. You don't need to know anything about margins, pilcrows, headers and footers etc and you can format into an epub file for e-books and pdf for print.

SOFTWARE: Then there's paid software like Vellum and Atticus, which automatically format the book for you, creating pdf and ePub files and give your book an ultra-professional finish. Vellum is only accessible via an Apple Mac or Mac-in-Cloud from a PC. If you want to investigate Vellum further, my blog, You Don't Need a Mac To Use Vellum! shows how you can use Vellum on your PC. I now use Atticus, which is the brainchild of Dave Chesson and is an amazing piece of software. It has a large array of features without being overwhelming and is sensibly priced compared to Vellum.

The team at Chas Cann Publishers can help you with reasonably priced, professional formatting services.

Formatting a Kindle Book on Word

Please, please, please ensure you proofread and edit your book before you go down the formatting route. Make certain that you have no more corrections to make! I've learned from the school of hard knocks and I don't want you to have to do the same too! It is a monumental waste of time and energy to make changes - particularly large alterations - after you've already formatted your entire book.

The style of genres is important to note here because the formatting of a modern Romance fiction book is going to differ from a Keto Diet Cookbook. Look at some of the best-sellers in your genre and check out how they look. For example, what style of font? Is it a serif or sans-serif font? What do the Chapter Headings tell you about these books? How does the start of each paragraph look? Note the different format features throughout the entire book. Readers will expect a certain genre to be formatted correctly. If it's not, when they take a peek at the 'Look Inside', they may be disappointed and move on to the next book.

Before you format, you'll need to rid your Word document of any unintentional errors that may have crept in whilst you were writing. For example, if you've used the Tab key, this will not transfer well to a Kindle e-reader. So, to de-format your manuscript, this is what you do. Copy and paste your manuscript into a new Word document and save. Go to 'Styles' on the 'Home' tab and click the icon below the up and down arrows. Click on 'Clear Formatting' and 'Save'. This will remove features such as bold, italics, images etc.

Turn on the pilcrow or paragraph symbol ¶ on the 'Home' tab. This will highlight formatting symbols so you can see, as you go along, if there are any problems brewing. For instance, a dot between words signifies a space. If you can see three dots between a pair of words, you know you will have to rectify it.

The instructions that follow are a basic introduction to Kindle formatting that may or may not work for your genre. What follows will give you a 'feel' of formatting which you can adjust to fit your genre.

Margins

Layout>Page Setup>Margins>Custom Margins. For e-books, choose 0.5" for Top, Bottom, Left and Right. Don't alter the Gutter setting (0) or Gutter position (Left).

Indentation and Line Spacing

On the 'Home' tab, go to 'Paragraph' and click on the di-agonal arrow in a box. Under 'General', it's usual to go for 'Justified' and 'Body Text'. 'Justified' means that your book looks neater overall because there is not a ragged effect on the right-hand side of every page.

Below 'Indentation' under 'Special', choose 'First Line' and alter the setting to '0.2'.

In the 'Spacing' section, go to 'Line Spacing', 'Multiple' at '1.2'.

Chapter Titles

The convention for e-books is to start each chapter on a new page. Apply 'Heading 1' to each chapter by placing your cursor before the first letter of the title, click 'Heading 1' on the 'Home' tab, and centre align it. If you have any sub-chapter headings, you can do the same but use 'Heading 2' instead. These will then automatically show up in the 'Table of Contents'.

Page Breaks

You can add a page break where you want a new page to start. Simply place your cursor where you want a new page to begin, go to 'Insert' on the menu bar and click 'Page Break' in the 'Pages' grouping.

Hyperlinks

Type in your link, which, for example, could be a website. Highlight it and go to 'Insert' on the menu bar. In the 'Links' section, click on 'Link', then 'OK' and you now have a clickable link. If you want to highlight a word/s and link them to a blog post, website etc., highlight the word/s, go to 'Insert' and click 'Link' in the 'Links' section. In the address box, paste the link and click 'OK'. Now when someone clicks on that grouping, they'll be directed away to the place you intended.

Images

Images need to be high quality (300 dpi or dots per inch) but also, because you are paying for the size of the e-book file, you need to compress each image. This minimises the size in bytes of a graphics file without altering the image to an unacceptable level. You can do this using free software at https://tinyjpg.com/

To insert an image, first place your cursor where you intend the image to go, then go to 'Insert' on the menu bar, 'Pictures' in the 'Illustrations' group, 'Insert Picture From' - 'This Device' for images saved to your computer or 'Online Pictures'. Find the compressed image you want to select and double-click it so that it appears in your document. If you need to adjust the size, go to 'Size' grouping in the top right-hand corner and alter the measurements so that the image is the right size for your page.

Front and Back Matter

Front matter in an e-book generally comprises:

- Title page including subtitle and author

- Copyright

- Dedication

- Contents

- Reader Magnet offer. The chapter entitled 'Marketing Basics' has more information on this subject.

The back matter usually includes:

- A 'thank you' and review prompt page. Reviews are critical to your book's success, so ask for one here and leave a hyperlink to your book's review page to make it easy for the reader

- Insert your Reader Magnet details again

- A chance for folks to join the Advance Readers Club (see Chapter 15)

- A preview of your next book. Especially important if you have a series. You could add a teaser chapter here from your sequel

- An author bio helps the reader connect to you as the author

- A listing for some or all of your other books available on Amazon. Here's your chance to sell more books organically by advertising them for free in the back of your book

One of the advantages of using a company called Geniuslink is to help you to secure sales that you otherwise might have lost and to capitalise on affiliate links. How does this work? If I place a direct link to Amazon.co.uk for one of my books in the back matter, whoever clicks that link, wherever they are in the world, will be directed to Amazon UK, which may not be their native site. But Geniuslink will re-direct them to their own Amazon site automatically, which means they are more likely to purchase your book. Geniuslink will also add an affiliate code from Amazon Associates (the affiliate arm of Amazon) to your link so that you can earn an extra income from this source.

Table of Contents

Creating a 'Table of Contents' is one of the last things you do. With a Kindle e-book, you need to have a 'Contents' page that's clickable so that readers can move effortlessly to any chapter by just clicking on it.

Go to 'References' in the menu bar, 'Table of Contents' (far left), 'Custom Table of Contents', untick 'Show Page Numbers'. You don't need page numbers with an e-book. Under 'General' and 'Formats', you can choose the TOC that you feel is most suitable for your book. 'Show Levels' allows you to show whichever 'Heading' levels you want to up to nine levels. You may want to show just 'Heading 1' so you would select '1'. Be sure to tick 'Use Hyperlinks Instead of Page Numbers' as this is required for all Kindle readers. Click 'OK' and 'Save'.

Preview

To ensure your document is going to look fine on a Kindle e-reader, upload your book to Kindle Previewer (https://www.amazon.com/Kindle-Previewer/b?ie=UTF8&node=21381691011).

Formatting a Paperback on Word

Please read the first four paragraphs under Kindle e-book formatting in the last section. They apply equally to print formatting. I would suggest, once you initially unformat your Kindle copy, to make another copy for your paperback. At least you'll know it's clear of anything unwanted.

In this section, I'm going to give you a basic introduction to formatting a print book in Word with no bleed. Bleed is where you want an image/s to extend right to the very edge of your page. This requires different margin and trim sizes.

Trim Size

Layout>Page Setup>Size>More Paper Sizes>

This relates to the physical size of your book. Popular trim sizes are 5" x 8" and 6" x 9". Whatever you do, don't change your mind about this once you've finished formatting because - you've guessed it – you'll have to do much of the formatting all over again, which is a headache you can do without!

Margins

This section relates to the space at the top, bottom, left and right of a page. With print versions, the margins of the book nearest the spine will need to be bigger than the outside margins because of the binding.

Layout>Page Setup>Margins>Custom Margins

The measurements under 'Margins' vary according to the tastes of each individual author but you can't go far wrong with 'Top and Bottom' 1", 'Right' margin 0.5" but the 'Left' (Inside or Gutter margin) will depend on the overall number of pages in your book so you'll need to use the <u>KDP Margin Guide</u>.

Front Matter:

We can classify front matter as everything in your book before the main body of text, including:

Half-Title Page

This includes just the title of the book and is placed on a right-hand page.

Title Page

The title, sub-title and author name appear here, always on a right-hand page.

Copyright

This is always on a left-hand page and, at its most basic, will include the © symbol, name of author or publisher, the ISBN and 'All Rights Reserved'.

Dedication

If you dedicate the book to someone, add the details here. This goes on a right-hand page.

Contents

The 'Contents' page begins on a right-hand page but may spread over a few pages.

Reader Magnets

I touch on Reader Magnets in a later chapter on Marketing Basics.

Add a section break here. This is a nifty device that creates a section that can be formatted independently from the rest of the document. Go to 'Layout' in the menu bar, click on 'Breaks' and under 'Section Breaks', hit 'Next Page'.

Body:

Chapter Title

Highlight your first chapter title. Click 'Heading 1' in 'Styles'. Instead of having to change every chapter in your book, right click on 'Heading 1', click 'Modify' and you can adjust the size of your chapter headings in terms of fonts, font sizes, adding bold, italics and underlined, etc. This will change every chapter heading in your book, saving time and effort.

Sub-Headings

You can use 'Heading 2' for subtitles. There are several title headings under 'Styles', so take a moment and see how they all look.

Body Text

Writers can choose drop capitals, indents and other formatting tools to begin a paragraph to increase the styling of a book. Certain genres require specific formatting. For example, drop caps are rarely used in non-fiction.

Back Matter:

Review Request

I always include a page where I ask readers for a review. If you don't ask, you don't get! You can ask your readers to leave a review on Amazon or, alternatively, you can select the URL for a review page in your most popular market/s and create a QR code. All you need to add to the following URL is your ASIN after the = sign. For the US, use this URL: **www.amazon.com/review/create-review?&asin**=. Go to Kindlepreneur QR Code Generator, paste your URL and add a logo if you want to. Then download for free. Your reader can now scan this code on their device to link direct to the review page, making the whole process far easier.

Just add your ASIN after the equals sign, and the link is complete for anyone reviewing in America. Alter to **.co.uk** for UK readers or whatever applies to where you live.

Author Bio

Your author bio is a small piece a couple of paragraphs long, complete with a head-shot photo. (For more on author bios, see 'Author Central' under 'Marketing Basics')

ARC Team

I always have an invitation in my books for people to join my 'Advance Readers Club'. I'm looking for people to review my new books prior to being published. The larger my team, the more reviews I'll get, which will give my books a head start on launch days. ARCs are covered in more depth in Chapter 15.

Other Books

The back matter is a great place to advertise your other books. If you're a fiction writer and people have loved your book, this gives them a chance to purchase others in a series. You might even include a sample chapter to whet their appetites....

In my print books, I use QR codes to make the readers' experience as easy as it can be if they're looking to buy a book here. Geniuslink (as mentioned in 'Formatting a Kindle Book on Word') also supply QR codes in their package.

Links

I'm now putting 'Link' pages in my books, where this is relevant for paperback/hard cover readers. Whereas with a Kindle book, you can easily add hyperlinks to connect to other places on the web, with a print book, that's not an option. The idea is to collate all the links that I've used in my book on one website page and then just place one link in my book directing readers to it. Once people are there, they can click on any links that look interesting.

Bibliography

This refers to all the sources you've used to research your work.

Images

To add an image, place your cursor where you want the image to go, head to 'Insert' in the menu bar, 'Pictures', 'Insert Picture From This Device' (if the image is on your PC). Double-click the image and it'll appear in your document.

Table of Contents

Creating a 'Table of Contents' is one of the last things you do.

Go to 'References' in the menu bar, 'Table of Contents' (far left), 'Custom Table of Contents', ensure 'Show Page Numbers' is ticked. Under 'General' and 'Formats', you can choose the TOC that you feel is most suitable for your book. 'Show Levels' allows you to show whichever heading levels you want to. You may want to show just 'Heading 1' so you select '1'. Untick 'Use Hyperlinks Instead of Page Numbers' as hyperlinks aren't necessary with print versions. Click 'OK' and 'Save'.

Export

When you're happy with your formatting, it's time to make a couple of adjustments and then copy your Word doc into a pdf file.

File>Options>Save

Scroll down to 'Preserve Fidelity When Sharing This Document'. Tick 'Embed The Fonts in this File' and untick the other boxes below.

Go to 'Advanced' (on the left-hand side of the box). Scroll down to 'Image Size and Quality'. Tick 'Do not Compress Images in File' box and ensure you place 330ppi in the 'Default Resolution' drop-down box. Press 'OK'.

Next, go to 'File' in the menu bar, 'Export' and then click on 'Create PDF/XPS'. Then 'Options' and tick 'PDF/A' if that hasn't already been done. Then click 'OK' and 'Publish'.

9
EDITING

OK, so I admit it! I've always loved learning about grammar, punctuation and spellings ever since I was a young lad, but, I hasten to add, that doesn't mean I'm perfect! It's not unknown for writers to get nervous around semi-colons, apostrophes, proper nouns and so on. On the other side of the coin, I used to hate mathematics with a vengeance getting a Grade 9 in my GCE 'O' Level. For younger readers, a Grade 9 was the worst you could attain. No matter how many people enthused and drooled over fractions and algebraic formulas, it bored me rigid! So, I get it when folk get frustrated and demoralised with the intricacies of the English language. It's not everyone's cup of tea!

That's why editors are worth their weight in gold. The most important characteristic of an editor is attention to detail, closely followed by an in-depth knowledge of grammar and style. They will make comments on the good and not-so-good aspects of your book and won't be afraid of hurting your feelings. Just remember they are critiquing your work objectively.

They will take your book and transform it into what the reader wants. Readers want well edited books that have been purged of 99.9% of all silly mistakes. Surely, that's what you would expect of a book too if you were buying one! One editor who used to work in traditional publishing said that every manuscript went through no less than four different editors and sometimes close to twelve rounds of editing. Believe it or not, even then, a few 'typos' still got through!

The fee for a good editor starts around $300.

Let's have a look at different types of editors:

Developmental Editor

They look at the overall picture looking to analyse structure, plot and characters in works of fiction and rhetorical concerns, organisation and flow of ideas in non-fiction.

Content Editor

A Content Editor will analyse the existing content in the book itself, referring to paragraph flow, tense, voice and readability. All editing is subjective. What one editor may like, another may not. It is imperative that you hire a content editor who is a specialist in your genre.

Copy Editor

Copy Editors zero in on grammar, syntax, punctuation and clarity and may rework and revise certain sentences and paragraphs.

Proofreaders

Often the last editors in line who go through the complete manuscript with a fine toothcomb looking for any remaining errors.

Most editors won't charge an hourly rate. They charge per word in the manuscript or by page.

If you're starting on a strict budget, Fiverr offers services for practically any writing option that you care to think about, including editing and proofreading. These gigs (or services offered) come with varying degrees of expertise.

ProWritingAid is a smart piece of self-editing software that comes with a free option and I highly recommend it. It highlights all manner of punctuation, grammar, spelling errors and a lot more besides so that you can prepare your document before it goes to your editor.

10
PUBLISHING A KINDLE BOOK

Most indie authors derive most of their income from e-books. There is more profit because there's no printing or shipping. Readers can purchase an e-book immediately – there's no wait involved like there is with a print version and, of course, you're not restricted to bricks and mortar bookstores. Your e-book is available worldwide to anyone who has an internet connection.

Log in to your KDP account, click on '+ Create' and you'll then see the image overleaf.

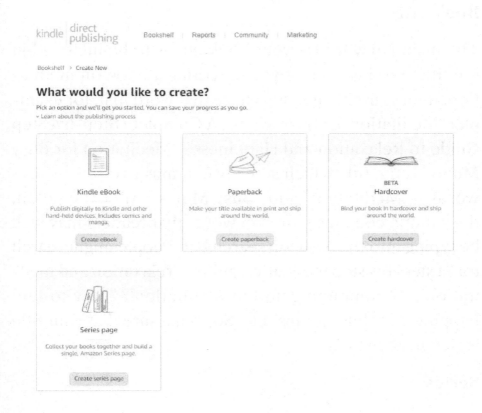

Click on 'Create eBook'. You now have three pages to complete before publishing your book and I'll take you through each of these step-by-step. Amazon often changes the look of these pages, so the sequence listed below may vary slightly.

KINDLE E-BOOK DETAILS

Language

This refers to the language in which your book is written.

Book Title

The main keyword for your book needs to be included in the title. For instance, if you're writing a book on meditation, then your title needs to have that word in it, for example: "Meditation for Busy Mums: A Complete Step-by-Step Guide to Relaxation and Happiness". "Meditation for Busy Mums" is the title which actually contains two sets of keywords - "Meditation" and "Busy Mums". After the colon, the subtitle contains more keywords that readers may well be typing into the Amazon search bar. People might search for "a step-by-step meditation guide", "relaxation and meditation", "a complete guide to meditation", "how to find happiness for busy mums" etc. So, make sure that your title is rich in keywords.

Series

If your book is part of a series, then to enable readers to find all the books, you need to link them together here but, if this is your first book, leave it blank.

Edition Number

If you've updated your initial book or made improvements, then highlight this by calling it a 2nd edition.

Author

This is where you put your actual name or a pen name.

Contributors

If you want to acknowledge anyone else like a co-author or translator, this is the place to include them.

Description

One of the awkward things about this section is that Amazon requires it in HTML code, which can be tricky to formulate. If you want to give it a go, then use this link: https://kdp.amazon.com/en_US/help/topic/G201189630, which explains some of the more basic HTML codes required here. If you want to bypass the coding, then check out Dave Chesson's 'Book Description Generator', which does most of the hard work for you. Copy and paste the Word doc containing the description into the Generator, make any changes you need to within the software and then 'Copy the Code'. Paste it into this box here on KDP and it's done!

Publishing Rights

My guess is that this is your work and not a public domain book, which is one that is out of copyright. Mark the box that shows that you hold the copyright.

Primary Audience

This is where you have to divulge whether your book contains sexually explicit images/text or not. Although the

Reading Age is optional, if you're writing books for children, you'll need to show the appropriate ages here.

Primary Marketplace

This is the country where you expect most of your sales will come from.

Categories

Amazon asks you to find three categories for your book. As we've already highlighted in 'Metadata and Why It's So Important', Amazon itself has a vast array of categories and it's important to choose those that are relevant to your book and genre.

Keywords

Keywords, as we've already seen, are those words that readers will enter into the Amazon search bar looking for your book. So, what words or phrases apply to your book? Spend some time collating these. You need to find seven but don't repeat any words that you've placed in your title or subtitle, because Amazon use these.

Pre-Order

Pre-orders work well for books in a series. Imagine reading a gripping thriller and loving every second. You'll be wanting the next book in the series and if it's not already out there to purchase, the next best thing is to pre-order.

KINDLE E-BOOK CONTENT

Manuscript

Kindle Create. I've tried Kindle Create and found it very limiting indeed. For me, it's too basic with few options but this is the section where you upload it, if you've chosen to utilise it.

Digital Rights Management (DRM). DRM is supposed to prevent unauthorised sharing and copying but this is questionable. I always go for 'No' under this heading. Apart from anything else, it has no impact on book sales and it allows my book to be shared.

Upload e-Book Manuscript. It does what it says on the can! Until June 2021, a MOBI file was the preferred choice for Amazon, but this is no longer required. Amazon accepts Word docx, ePub and KPF (Kindle Create) files. While you can certainly upload a Word docx file, an ePub file has certain characteristics that make it more rewarding for the reader. To change a Word document to ePub, there's free software like <u>Calibre</u> or paid options such as Atticus.

Kindle e-Book Cover

Upload Your Cover Here. If you're looking to sell large quantities of books, then I don't suggest you use Cover Creator unless you have a background in book design. Most

DIY book covers stand out for all the wrong reasons! Your cover has to be a JPG or TIFF file.

AI Generated Content

Amazon now require authors to declare whether they have used AI-generated content (text, images or translations). This is because Amazon are seeing an avalanche of AI produced books by people hoping to make a quick buck. But AI is nothing new. Many writers have been using it for years in the form of software, for example. So, in order to clarify the situation, Amazon distinguishes between **AI-generated** and **AI-assisted** content. In essence, if you use AI to generate text, images or translations, then you have to declare it.

However, according to Amazon guidelines, you do not have to disclose AI-assisted content. This is defined as using AI-based tools 'to brainstorm and generate ideas' or 'to edit, refine, error-check, or otherwise improve that content (whether text or images)'. As long as you have created the text and images yourself.

AI can be seen as a curse or a blessing. The free version of Chat GPT is an excellent tool for creating book descriptions and ad copy, which come within the AI-assisted guidelines above. But AI will continue to divide the author community, particularly as it becomes even more powerful.

Kindle e-Book Review

Once uploaded, you can look at the finished article and amend not only any errors that Amazon may want you to make but also to ensure there are no formatting or other mistakes. You can download 'Kindle Previewer' on to your PC and this will basically do the same thing so you can check your book before uploading.

Kindle e-Book ISBN

An ISBN is optional with Kindle. If you're planning to go wide with your distribution (i.e. not stick exclusively to Amazon) then supplying your own ISBN will pay dividends later.

KINDLE E-BOOK PRICING

KDP Select Enrollment

The choice is yours whether or not to go exclusive with Amazon, which, if you do, means you're not able to sell your e-book anywhere else (including your website).

By enrolling with KDP Select, you have the options of its Free 5-day Promotion and Countdown deals. You can also make money from KENP reads, which is where you earn a royalty for the number of pages read by those who've sub-scribed to Kindle Unlimited. This is a subscription service where readers pay a monthly fee in exchange for access to any number of Kindle books.

Territories

In most cases, the Worldwide option is the one to choose. 'Individual Territories' would be used if, say, you had a traditional publishing deal in the US only and you decided to self-publish in the UK.

Primary Marketplace

This is the country where you believe you'll make the most sales.

Pricing, Royalty and Distribution

Books priced between $2.99 and $9.99 attract a 70% royalty. Outside of these parameters, it's 35%. Remember that you also have to pay a delivery fee when readers upload your book, but you only pay this on the 70% royalty. If your book is image-heavy, then your delivery fee will be higher and maybe by reducing your royalty rate to 35%, and hence avoid the delivery fee, you may be better off financially.

When you load your price into the US price box, it auto-populates all the other countries with an equivalent price. You need to check that prices in these countries end with .99 or .49 which is what readers expect. Just to be on the safe side, it's also prudent to check your actual royalties in all these countries to ensure you're not under-pricing.

Terms and Conditions

These are the T and Cs that you're signing up for when you publish your e-book.

Draft/Publish

If you're not planning to publish yet, click 'Save As Draft' until you're ready to present your work to the world. When you do publish, there is a formal review process than can take up to 72 hours and then your book will be live. When your e-book goes live, download a copy to check that it looks presentable. Ensure that you reduce the price to its lowest component, buy your copy and raise the price again.

11
PUBLISHING A PAPERBACK BOOK

Before you can publish your paperback, you will need to have your book cover completed along with your back cover blurb, which is the text you want to use on the back cover. Usually, it's the same as the book description because both are doing the same job – tempting the reader to make the sale. If you've already tackled your Kindle e-book, you'll have already created your book description.

OK, so log in to your KDP account, click on '+ Create' and then 'Create paperback'. As with the Kindle e-book, you now have three pages to complete and I'll take you through each of these step-by-step. Amazon often changes the layout of these pages so it may not follow the same sequence exactly.

PAPERBACK DETAILS

This section is the same as the one to create a Kindle e-book except for the last two items:

Publication Date and **Release Date**. Both these are actually the same dates. With 'Release Date' you can delay releasing your book up to 5 to 90 days in advance. Don't confuse this with a pre-order, which is only permitted with e-books. I just leave these two boxes blank because I'll be publishing my book straight away. Amazon will automatically add both these dates when your book goes live.

PAPERBACK CONTENT

Print ISBN

KDP will supply you with a free ISBN, which is fine if you want to keep with Amazon and not branch out with other retailers offline or online. If your plan is **not** to be exclusive to Amazon in the future, it's better to purchase your own.

Print Options

Ink and Paper Type

In this section, you can opt for different paper interiors and colour types. Authors will often print fiction on cream paper, which is usually easier on the eye, while non-fiction is usually printed on white paper. You have a choice of colour. Amazon print standard colour on lighter paper using ink-jet printers and is more suitable for larger books. Premium colour is best for smaller image-heavy books like children's books. You will get more sharpness and clarity with premium colour.

Trim Size

This is the finished size of your book. These can vary from genre to genre. For my joke books, I use 6" x 9" and for other non-fiction books I'll normally go for 5" x 8". Check out what trim sizes your competitors use.

Bleed Settings

If you want some or all of the images in your book to extend to the edge of the page after trimming, you'll need to select bleed.

Paperback Cover Finish

You have the choice of Matte or Glossy. My preference is glossy, but it's entirely up to you.

Manuscript

This is where you upload your pdf file. Amazon will only accept this type of file. If you've used Word to create your manuscript, you can easily convert it in Word to a pdf file as described under 'Formatting a Paperback on Word' in Chapter 8.

Book Cover

Use Cover Creator

You can use Amazon's free Cover Creator or upload your own. I have never used this software because my preference is for a professional finish.

Upload a Cover You Already Have

Pro designers know they need to supply a cover in PDF mode. This includes the front, spine and back cover, where a small white space for your ISBN details/barcode is required.

AI Generated Content

The same applies here as it does to an e-book.

Book Preview

Launch Previewer

Amazon may highlight some errors that will need correcting before you can proceed. By checking each page, you may also note other mistakes that need attending to.

Summary

This is basically a checklist of your print options together with a page count. Note the printing costs on the right-hand side.

PAPERBACK RIGHTS AND PRICING

Territories

All Territories

Select this box if you hold all the rights to your book for worldwide distribution. If this is your first book, select this option.

Individual Territories

Traditionally published authors may have sold the rights to their book in the US, which means they can self-publish anywhere else in the world.

Primary Marketplace

Consider from which geographical location you would expect most of your sales to come.

Pricing Royalty and Distribution

Taking each column in turn:

Marketplace lists every country where your book will be available.

List Price. If your 'Primary Marketplace' is the US, then the US dollar price will be the first country in the 'Marketplace' (above). All other currencies will be based on this dollar figure automatically.

I like to set my prices ending in .49 or ideally .99 so I wouldn't want my UK price, for example, ending up something like £7.21. So, I go into each list price and change them manually. When doing this, keep a keen eye on your actual royalties in every country, ensuring they are adequate and giving you a good return.

The Untitled Column shows the cost of your book once local taxes are added.

Printing highlights the printing cost in each individual country's currency.

Amazon Rate/Royalty – these two columns show the royalty rate and the amount you can expect from each sale. Amazon calculates the royalty by multiplying the royalty rate by the list price less the printing costs. So, if your paperback retails for $6.99 and the print cost is $1.93, you'll earn $2.26. (0.60 x 6.99 – 1.93 = 2.26).

Expanded Distribution – if you select this, it enables you to receive a lesser royalty rate where Amazon distributes your book beyond Amazon itself. If you decide to publish your book with another platform such as Ingram Spark (see the later chapter 'Going Wide'), this option won't be available to you but, in my opinion, the benefits of having an alternative source of income and distribution outweigh the minimal advantages of staying with Expanded Distribution.

Terms and Conditions

Remember when you click 'Publish Your Paperback Book' you are bound by Amazon's Terms and Conditions and your book will then be available within the next 72 hours.

Request a Book Proof

Book proofs aren't the same as copies bought from Amazon. Proofs have an inferior quality and have a 'Not for Resale' watermark running through the entire book. They cost the same as ordering an actual author copy.

When your book goes live, head for your KDP dashboard, find your book, click on the ellipsis beside 'Paperback Actions' and click on 'Order Author Copies'. Check through the book when it arrives to make sure there are no errors.

12
CREATING AN AUDIOBOOK

Even though the numbers of audio books being sold are far smaller than e-books or print versions, audio books are the fastest growing area in the publishing marketplace, so it's a good time to dip your toes in and get started.

Where do I go to self-publish my audio book?

1. ACX or Audiobook Creation Exchange (www.ACX .com) is owned by Amazon, allowing you to sell your audio books on Amazon, Audible and iTunes. Royalties depend on whether or not you sign an exclusivity deal. If you limit your audio book to ACX alone, then you can expect a higher royalty. By doing this, you are limiting your reach. Admittedly, Amazon itself is a large market, but there is a wider global scope out there, including libraries that aren't served by ACX. Exclusive rights on ACX means your commission rate is 40%; non-exclusivity reduces the rate to 25%.

2. New kids on the block like Findaway Voices and

<u>Kobo Audio</u> are powering forward, offering direct competition with ACX.

You can find narrators on these sites, or look elsewhere. What sort of voice do you need? Male or female? African, Caucasian, Eastern? Softly spoken or more gritty? Indeed, you may want to create the audio file yourself. But what may seem relatively easy in theory can become more of a challenge in reality. Of course, the author can do it and many do so. Whereas you or I might inadvertently include police sirens or low-flying jets in the background of our audio, professional narrators won't allow that to happen. Professionals will also maintain their momentum throughout. You and I might noticeably start flagging towards the end of a particularly long chapter. If we have to stop and start again in the middle of a chapter, will it sound seamless? If you feel confident and your voice fits, there's nothing to stop you.

Contract options can vary. You usually pay narrators per finished audio hour (i.e. if the audio tape is 4 hours long, you pay for those 4 hours) and you keep the royalty. Payment per finished hour is around $200. Alternatively, with ACX, you can halve the royalty with the narrator, meaning no money passes between you and the narrator until the book starts selling. This helps if you're on a tight budget and would find the upfront fee a little daunting.

13
PRE-ORDERS

A pre-order is where you make your book available on Amazon prior to publication. Readers purchase it up to one year in advance. This works really well if you're writing a series because imagine a reader is bowled over by your first book, they'll be itching to get their hands on your next offering. Pre-ordering allows them to do this with readers receiving their books on launch day. At the time of writing, Amazon is only allowing e-books to be pre-ordered.

The length of the pre-order period is important because the Amazon algorithm counts the pre-order on the day of the order. So, having a long pre-order period hampers your efforts to maintain a high ranking because they calculate your book sales over a longer period. You need to be looking at a shorter period aligned to other marketing activities to keep momentum going and the rankings high.

Many authors add teasers to the end of a book to tempt readers to purchase the next one in the series. They will willingly sign up for a book on pre-order if they've enjoyed the first. In this world of instant gratification, pre-orders are often harder to market. Offering your readers a few chapters of the new book when they pre-order and even offering a free copy of your book in a draw to all those who have pre-ordered, will keep their interest high before they actually receive the book on their device.

Amazon needs the book to be uploaded on to their platform 72 hours before the pre-order is due to launch. Failure to do this means your pre-order will be cancelled and you won't be able to offer another e-book on pre-order for one year. This also applies to cancelling a pre-order, so it's as well to make absolutely sure that your deadline date is achievable.

14
GOING WIDE

What Does 'Going Wide' Mean?

The biggest bookseller in the world is Amazon, but it's not the only one!

As I've mentioned already, when you sell your e-books in book outlets outside Amazon, you cannot benefit from KDP Select. If you are a first-time author, I would start with KDP Select until you find your feet. As a result, you will access royalties from Kindle Unlimited and be able to organise Countdown and 5 Day Free Promotions. This applies to your e-books only. You can start going wide with your paperbacks whenever you wish.

There is a whole, huge book distribution network out there that doesn't involve Amazon directly at all. I know this book is primarily about publishing on Amazon, but I've added this chapter in case you decide to investigate the global opportunities that this affords.

Print On Demand

Print On Demand has revolutionised the production of books. If I want to order one book online, I can now do so and receive that single copy in no time at all. Before the internet came along, books were printed in bulk and then shipped to bricks and mortar book stores where buyers would congregate. The worldwide web changed all that.

Let's have a look at Ingram Spark, which is the world's largest book wholesaler and distributes to 40,000 retailers globally, including online, bricks and mortar bookshops like Barnes & Noble and Waterstones, and the library market. It's fairly simple to upload your books on to this platform. In 2023, Ingram stopped charging set-up fees, so it is now free to upload your e-book or paperback. However, if you need to change anything once you've published, then there is a revision fee of $25. At the time of writing this 2nd edition, if you're a member of the Alliance of Independent Authors, you're able to get these charges waived, which is a tremendous bonus. Ingram Spark has been the Print On Demand choice for many authors who want the widest market for their books.

Don't forget if you chose a free ISBN with Amazon, this will not be acceptable anywhere else, so you will need to purchase your own for publishing with Ingram Spark or any other POD company like Draft2Digital Print, which, as I write, is in its beta stages but should be available internationally soon.

With Ingram, you can discount your book up to 55% and decide on whether you want the hassle and cost of dealing with returns. Choosing the highest discount will typically get your book into more stores, and a 'No Return' policy will save a lot of headaches.

Personally, I used to have all my e-books and paperbacks solely on KDP but I'm now uploading my print titles to Ingram Spark. As much as I enjoy the KDP experience, I don't want to have all my eggs in the Amazon basket. For starters, Amazon can change their guidelines/terms and conditions without warning, which could harm my business. Second, I want the widest reach possible for all my books.

My '1001 One-Liners and Dad Jokes' series attracts a good number of KENP reads. If you remember, when you sign up for KDP exclusivity in KDP Select, you attract royalties from folk who've taken out Kindle Unlimited subscriptions. This is based on the number of pages read by subscribers. These joke e-books do really well, attracting around $250 per month in KENP royalties alone, so I am reticent about coming out of KDP Select for these titles. However, with my other non-fiction e-books that don't attract such high KENP reads, I am starting to market these through the aggregator Draft2Digital (D2D). Aggregators are companies that will take your e-book and then distribute it as widely as they are able. D2D will take a percentage cut from the sales of your books. Other aggregators include Smash-words, PublishDrive and Street Lib.

Digital Outlets

Kobo is a Canadian digital book company (e-books and audiobooks) which was bought by Rakuten in 2012 with a reach into 170 countries around the globe. Kobo Writing Life is their self-publishing platform. What makes Kobo somewhat different is that it is all about books and nothing else.

Apple needs no introduction. As part of a worldwide brand, the Apple Books app is automatically pre-installed on every iPhone produced. The Apple Books app is available in 51 countries. If you publish direct, you'll receive a 70% royalty for books priced from $0.99.

Google Play is another of the principal players in the digital book market and is available in 75 countries.

Nook is the digital alternative to the Barnes and Noble bookstores in the US. It's also the name of their e-reader device. It's available only in the US but, despite that, it's a force to be reckoned with.

15
MARKETING BASICS

Marketing can be a thorny subject with some writers. Authors write. That's what they do! Where does marketing fit in?

Publishing your book is a great achievement. Marketing gets it in front of readers. There are many marketing strategies and, in this chapter, I've noted down a few that you could use in your marketing plan. It's important to remember just how critical marketing is to your overall strategy, so some time will have to be put aside to accommodate it.

The choice is whether you break up your day into, say, writing in the morning when you're at your freshest and other jobs, including marketing, in the afternoons. This works well for most authors. Time management is essential and what works for one person may well be anathema to another, so finding your own workplan and, above all, sticking to it, is something your future writer self will thank you for!

Email List

In order to build an extensive business, creating an email list is a top priority. The major thrust of it is to offer something of value **for free** in exchange for readers' email addresses.

You will need an opt-in offer, an email service provider and, if you don't have your own website, a landing page. The opt-in offer (or freebie) could be a workbook, cheat sheet, e-book, how-to video, or anything that your readers would find irresistible. An email service provider will supply the mechanics of building your subscriber list, sending out newsletters, automated responses, etc. Some will offer their services for free until you reach a certain number of subscribers. I use Mailerlite which is user friendly and has all the features you'll need in their free option.

The best way to engage with your list is to contact them regularly. Get them excited about you and your brand. Regular contact is essential and I recommend reaching out at least once a month. I send a newsletter out every week to my '1001 One-Liners Club'. The intention here is to give all my subscribers something to laugh about every Monday morning, which is traditionally not the best day of the week for most people! I just created a simple landing page with Mailerlite. When someone leaves their email address, it's added to my list automatically.

If your reader magnet is an e-book, I recommend <u>Book-Funnel</u>, who will deliver it automatically to whoever signs up for it. It's also useful for sending books to your ARC team (see below) in order to get reviews.

Why is all this so important? Whenever someone buys a book of yours from Amazon, **they** keep the reader's details, such as their email address. This is a way of obtaining some of those email addresses, which, once you have them, they are yours! You can ask your subscribers for reviews, you can send out details of your new books to them and have a ready-built fan base, plus you can keep engaging with them to build an army of super fans.

ARC Team

Sales of your book rely on 'social proof'. This is where prospective readers will go to reviews to see what other readers have made of your book. If the reviews are good compared to similar books, the one with the best reviews will usually secure the sale.

Building an ARC, Advance Readers Club team (also known as Advance Reader Copies or Advance Review Copies) will help in your efforts to get some excellent reviews at the launch of your book and therefore influencing others to buy. It takes time to build such a team. One way to start is to ask readers to join your team by including a page in the back matter of your book. You explain that you'll send a free e-book to them (about two weeks prior to the launch) and to ask them to leave a review on Amazon once they've read it. Do not imply that you are giving them a free book **in exchange for** a review. Amazon does not like it when authors pay or exchange something of value for a review. You may risk having your account terminated.

Be aware that in order to leave a review, members of your team need to have spent £40 ($50) on Amazon products using a valid debit or credit card in the previous twelve months.

Reviews

There are a number of ways to secure reviews for your book. The ARC team and email list mentioned above are really effective ways of getting more reviews.

As I've mentioned briefly earlier, ask for them in your back matter and give them an easy access link to the Customer Review page. I generally use two links – one to the Customer Review section in the US; the other to the UK. You can explain how important reviews are to independent authors like yourself. Why not include an informal photo of yourself with your family and/or pets to show that you are a living breathing human being with emotions and feelings? Let them know that you always read the reviews.

However tempting it might be to respond to a one star review, don't do it. Even Stephen King has had one star reviews. You'll never please all the people, all the time. On the other hand, don't ignore them. If you get enough poor reviews relating to one aspect of your book, then maybe you need to give it your attention. Likewise, I never respond to good reviews either. Discover what people like about your books and do more of the same.

Author Central

An often-overlooked part of the whole Amazon experience is Author Central, which has been created for you to sell more books. You can't set this up until you publish a book.

Setting up an Author Central page is easy to do. Go to <u>Author Central</u> and click 'Join For Free'. Use your KDP account to log in. The name you enter should be the one that is on the cover of your book. Claim your book/s and they will appear on your Author Central page. If they do not, then you will need to contact Amazon. Once your book is claimed, your account will be activated. Verify your account and you're on your way!

Amazon allows you three names on your account. For example, that could be your own name and two pen names.

1. Start With a Sizzling Bio

Get started under the 'Biography' tab. You should mention your books, credentials and some fun facts like this example from Victoria Schwab:

Victoria "V.E." Schwab is the #1 New York Times bestselling author of more than a dozen books, including the acclaimed Shades of Magic series, This Savage Song, Our Dark Duet, City of Ghosts and Vicious. Her work has received critical acclaim and has been featured in the New York Times, Entertainment Weekly, Washington Post, and more. When she's not haunting Paris streets or trudging up English hillsides, she lives in Nashville and is usually tucked in the corner of a coffee shop, dreaming up monsters.

If this is your first book, then don't worry. You won't have achieved best-seller status or professional accolades just yet! All you need to add is a resumé about yourself and your self-publishing journey so far. You can alter your bio at any time in the future. If you have them set up, don't forget to add your website, social media profiles and/or blogs to enable readers to find your presence outside Amazon.

Your bio should be at least 100 characters and once you're happy with it, just click 'Add Biography' and boom! You're there!

2. Add a Professional Photo

It's time to upload that photo of yourself. Ensure that it's a high quality, professionally produced profile. There's no need to limit yourself to just one photo – you can use up to eight! Some can be with you holding one of your books or attending literary events. Be creative! These additional photos don't need to be of the same quality as your main photo, but they still need to look good. Go to 'Profile' at the top of your Author Central dashboard and then scroll down and you'll see 'Photos and Videos' on the right-hand side.

3. Create a Shareable URL

This is available on your amazon.com page only.

You can create a URL that you can share on your website and social media platforms that will take your potential readers direct to your Author Central page. Surely that's worth doing! On your Author Central dashboard, go to 'Profile' at the top of the page and then on the right-hand side of the page, click on 'Author Page URL'. When you access this page, it'll give you the instructions to set up this useful link.

4. Add Your Blog Posts

This is available on your amazon.com page only.

Imagine how good it would be if you could connect to your readers with your latest blog posts via your Author Central page. Well, you can! Head over to 'Profile' at the top of your dashboard and over to your right, go to 'Manage blog feeds'. When you 'Add Feed', this is not your website URL – it's the RSS feed.

'Reports and Marketing' shows Sales Ranks of all books, a Book Scan report (US only) and Customer Reviews where you can see your book reviews in each country without having to go on to each country's sales page.

Author Website

These days, it doesn't cost a huge amount to set up your own website. Why do you need one? Once you've set up your own author website, you then have a presence on the internet and a place to send your readers to discover more about you. Not only that, but you'll have all your books listed on your site together with reader magnets offering something of value in exchange for their email addresses, which you will use to build your all-important email list.

Many entrepreneurial authors also sell their books direct from their websites with the added benefits of earning more from each sale and gaining the readers' email addresses.

Just a word of caution about free websites. These may be appealing when you first start out when budgets are tight, but, ultimately, your site never actually belongs to you. If the company that provides your website disappears without a trace, so does yours. Always get someone to host your website if you're able. <u>Bluehost</u> is very popular and reasonably priced.

Book Promotion Sites

There are large numbers of free book promotion websites where you can promote your books. You will need to set up a promotion on KDP Select and offer your book for free or a Countdown deal starting at 99c (99p).

Basically, you then upload details about your book and your offer to these sites. They have a website/Facebook group/newsletter comprising thousands of eager readers looking for a good deal. There's no guarantee that they'll feature your book but I've found that on average 5-10% of them will. You can pay for a guaranteed spot and these can vary in price and effectiveness.

If you want to save time <u>KDROI</u> is a piece of software that will do this job for you. You only have to enter your details once and KDROI will send your book details and offer to over 30 book promotion sites.

Why would you want to offer your book for free or at a discounted price?

These are great for launching your book. When I offered my book '1001 One-Liners and Short Jokes' for free at its launch in 2020 (under the KDP Select 5-day Free Promotion deal), it got 10,000 downloads, which catapulted the book to #1 best-seller in the Free Top 100 Best Sellers. It also got more reviews. My one regret was that I didn't understand about reader magnets at that time and couldn't capitalise on obtaining email addresses from a potential 10,000 readers! Since then, it's been a regular #1 best-seller on Amazon.

So, by offering your book at a discounted price (free promotions are best), you will find an improvement in your book's ranking, more reviews and more sign-ups to your email list.

Amazon Ads

When you search for books on Amazon, or anything else for that matter, you're likely to find the first one or two results are shown as 'Sponsored'. If you were to click on one of these, the seller would be charged even if you don't purchase the product. These are Amazon Ads and are often referred to as Pay-Per-Click (PPC) advertising. One of the great benefits is that your book, even though it's brand new with no sales history, can appear in the top three for that listing.

Promoting a book via Amazon Ads starts in KDP Bookshelf. At some stage, you may be prompted to add your bank details in order for Amazon to debit your account with any forthcoming advertising fees:

1. Find the ellipsis and click on 'Promote and Advertise' Choose 'Run an Ad Campaign' and select which country you wish to advertise in and then click 'Create an Ad Campaign'

2. Choose 'Sponsored Products'

3. In 'Settings', select a name for your campaign in addition to a start and end date

4. Set a daily budget (between $5 and $10 depending on your funds) which cannot be exceeded by Amazon

5. Set up 'Automatic Targeting' initially. This is where Amazon choose the keywords for you

6. Choose 'Dynamic Bids – Down Only' if this is your first foray into Amazon Ads. 'Dynamic Bids -Up and Down' is useful if you need a more aggressive campaign

7. Select 'Custom Text Ad' which gives you the chance to market with a message and image of your book

8. Click on the appropriate book

9. Set the default bid around 34p for the US (Halve that for the UK because it's a smaller market)

10. Write your ad copy in 'Custom Text'

11. 'Launch Campaign'

This is a fairly basic campaign to get you started. Three resources to help you further are:

- Dave Chesson's <u>free Amazon Ads Course</u>. This is an awesome course and one I thoroughly recommend to you.

- Bryan Cohen's <u>Author Ad School</u> (formerly Amazon Ad School) which was pivotal in changing our fortunes in our first year. Every quarter, Bryan hosts a Free 5-day Challenge, which I urge you to sign up for. It is intensive, but you will learn so much about how to set up and maintain Amazon Ads, which will be an integral part of your marketing strategy.

- Jules at <u>Chas Cann Publishers</u> is an expert Amazon Ads strategist. She turned our business around in 2020 from turning over £40 per month to £2500 per month within five months just using Amazon Ads! If you haven't got the time or patience to devote hours to learning how to set up and maintain them, contact Jules today. She offers a free 20 minute consultation on Zoom to discuss your needs. You'll be surprised how affordable it can be! info@chascannco.com for more details.

The one thing to remember is that you invest in Amazon Ads up front, but you don't get paid for the results of those ads for around two months. There's always a lag between paying out for the ads and receiving reimbursement through your royalties. Be sure that your cash flow will support this before you start out.

16
IN CONCLUSION

Self-publishing is not a get-rich-quick scheme. If you put into practice all that you've learnt in this book, it'll give you a massive head start.

Despite all the advice I can give in this manual, the key element will be the writing itself. If your first book doesn't perform as well as you expected, be prepared to analyse where the challenge lies and fix it. If you sense it may be your writing that's letting you down, there are many books and courses on how to write non-fiction and fiction. Always keep referring to this book and internalising the concepts and strategies. As long as you have passion and commitment, you will find the answers to any challenges you face. If other people can make money in this business, so can you!

Remember that you're not on your own.

Come and visit www.chascannco.com where you can find blogs on self-publishing, resources and competitive author services. You can contact me directly if you need any advice – info@chascannco.com. Our mission is to help new and aspiring indie authors make a success of their writing careers. You can follow us on <u>Facebook</u> where you'll find useful tips and relevant information.

In the meantime, I wish you every success with your writing career and I look forward to hearing from you about your future achievements.

Dream big!

Helpful Links

As stated in the Introduction, to make life a little easier, all the external web links have been underlined in the main text and listed by chapter at https://www.chascannco.com /links or scan the QR code below.

Helpful Links

May I ask a favour?

Thank you for reading *'How to Self-Publish on Amazon'* and I hope that you found it was of value to you.

If you liked the book and have a moment to spare, I'd be very grateful if you could leave a short review. They not only help other readers discover the kinds of books they want to read, but they also help support independent authors like myself. I read every review - they really do make a huge difference.

For readers from the USA and the UK, I've set up QR codes below that will take you direct to the Customer Review section of Amazon in your particular country.

USA READERS:

UK READERS:

About the Author

Graham Cann is a #1 best-selling author and CEO of Chas Cann Publishers. He began writing short stories over fifty years ago when he was about 8-years-old, followed by a couple of short novels. But the creative spark fizzled out in the years that followed, apart from a year's spell as editor of the Taverham Newsletter in the mid-1990s. It was some years later when he contacted a publisher with an idea for publishing twenty Norfolk countryside walks that the desire to write was reignited. The outcome was the *'Guide to Norfolk Pub Walks'*, which became the catalyst for his self-publishing career.

He set up Chas Cann Publishers in 2018 with the desire to help new and experienced writers with a range of sensibly priced author services.

DO YOU LIKE READING BOOKS?

WOULD YOU LIKE US TO SEND YOU FREE BOOKS?

Why not join our Advance Readers Club? All members receive free e-books on all sorts of interesting subjects which have included puppy care, cookbooks and joke books, prior to the book being marketed globally.

All we ask you to do is to read through it and then leave an honest review on Amazon.

Please contact us at info@chascannco.com to be added to our VIP list of readers or scan the QR code below. *Your email address is protected – it will never be divulged to third parties.*

A SELECTION OF BOOKS BY THE SAME PUBLISHER

For the full range of titles, please visit

www.chascannco.com

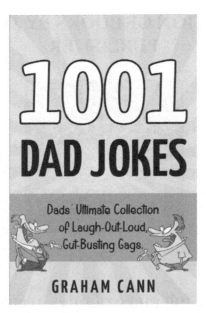

1001 Dad Jokes

The classic collection of the most hilarious dad jokes guaranteed to give you hours of laughter

SCAN THE QR CODE

Colour 'n Relax

Reconnect to your inner creativity, colouring your way to inner peace and calm

SCAN THE QR CODE

Mindfulness for Beginners: A Practical Guide to Finding Peace and Happiness in an Anxious World

This easy-to-understand guide empowers you to take control and bring contentment into your life

SCAN THE QR CODE

Made in United States
Orlando, FL
01 March 2024

44274862R00075